The Valentine's Day Joke Book

by Lisa Regan

SCHOLASTIC

New York • Toronto • London • Auckland
Sydney • Mexico City • New Delhi • Hong Kong

What do you call two birds in love?

Tweethearts!

What did the farmer give his wife on Valentine's Day?

Hogs and kisses!

What did the magnet say to the refrigerator?

"I find you very attractive!"

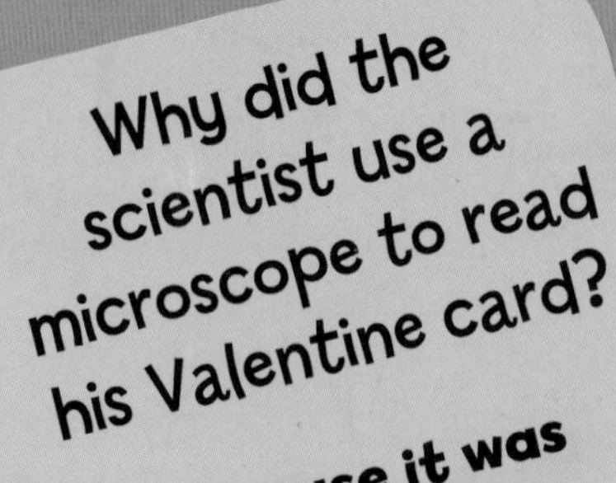

Why did the scientist use a microscope to read his Valentine card?

Because it was Valen-tiny!

Why do skunks love Valentine's Day?

Because they're scent-imental!

What did the dark chocolate say to the white chocolate?

"You're so sweet!"

Why did the bee fall in love?

Because his girlfriend was bee-you-tiful!

What did the elephant say to the chair?

"I've got a crush on you!"

What was the chef's secret ingredient for love?

Valenthyme!

Did you hear about the zombies that fancied each other?

It was love at first fright!

What message was inside the rabbit's Valentine card?

Some bunny loves you!

Why was Dr. Frankenstein never lonely?

Because he was good at making new friends!

Why did the girl put sugar under her pillow?

Because she wanted sweet dreams!

What did the caveman give to his wife to show he loved her?

Ugs and kisses!

Why did the boy take his girlfriend to the wrestling event?

He'd promised her a ring on their next date!

What did the orca say to his girlfriend?

"Whale you marry me?"

Why did the girl agree to date the baker?

Because she was dough-nuts about him!

What plans did the brick walls make for their date?

They arranged to meet at the corner!

What did the candy store owner write to her Valentine?

"We're mint for each other!"

Why did the girl fall in love with the goalie?

Her dad said he was a keeper!

Jim: Do you have a date for the Valentine Ball?

Jill: Yes, February 14th!

What did the algebra teacher write in her Valentine to the English teacher?

"How do I love thee? Let me count the ways..."

Did you hear about the crab that attended a Valentine dance?

It pulled a mussel!

Doctor, my date won't see me for medical reasons.

Did she say why?

Yes – I make her sick!

What did one teddy bear say to the other on Valentine's Day?

"I love you beary much!"

What did the smitten mitten say to the hand?

"You're the one that I glove!"

What kind of fruit loves chocolate?

A cocoa-nut!

What did the sheep say to his girlfriend?

"I love ewe!"

What did the rhino write in the Valentine's card?

"I love you a ton!"

Did you hear about the blood cells that fell in love?

Unfortunately it was all in vein.

Why is lettuce a very romantic food?

Because it's all heart!

How did the rabbit send his girlfriend a Valentine's card?

By hare mail!

What do monsters do at a wedding reception?

They toast the bride and groom!

Mindy: Whisper something soft and sweet to me.

Lewis: Er, melted chocolate?

Did you hear about the couple who met in a revolving door?

They're still going around together!

What did the snail write in the Valentine's card?

"Be my Valen-slime!"

Did you hear about the acrobats who were dating?

They were head over heels in love!

What did the vulture say when he asked a girl on a date?

"I've got a bone to pick with you!"

Did you hear about the history teachers who liked each other?

They enjoyed many dates together!

What flowers do squirrels give on February 14th?

Forget-me-nuts!

Did you hear about the kitty whose date never showed up?

It was a catastrophe!

Why did the raisin go out with a prune?

Because it couldn't get a date!

What did the Valentine card say to the postage stamp?

"Stick with me and we'll go places!"

What did the little baker write in his personal ad?

"Looking for someone short and sweet!"

What do you call a woman who is married to a hippy?

Mississippi!

Sally: I want to leave you, but I can't.

Michael: Are you afraid you will break my heart?

Sally: No, but you're sitting on my skirt.

Where did the sheep go on their honeymoon?

To the Baa-hamas!

Why did the cats fall in love?

Because they were purr-fect for each other!

What do bats do on a date?

They just hang out!

What did the firefly say at the end of the date?

"Got to glow now, but can I see you again?"

What did the cotton thread say to the needle?

"I reel-y admire your work!"

Did you hear about the unlucky porcupine that couldn't see very well?

It fell in love with a hairbrush!

What did the painter say to his girlfriend?

"I love you with all my art!"

Knock, knock!
Who's there?
Howard.
Howard who?
Howard you like to know who your secret admirer is?

What did the girl think on her first date with the undertaker?

"I've made a grave mistake!"

What did the ghost write in its Valentine card?

"I love yoooooouuuuu!"

Why did the pirate ask the kind girl on a date?

He'd heard she had a heart of gold!

What did the bacon say to the tomato?

"Lettuce get together!"

What did the loved-up calculator say?

"You can count on me!"

What did the octopus say to his date?

"Can I hold your hand hand hand hand hand hand hand hand?"

How did the ghosts travel on honeymoon?

By scareplane!

How did the knife persuade the loaf to go on a date?

It buttered it up!

Why did the man fall in love with the mermaid?

He liked girls with wavy hair!

Suzie Sheep: Do you love me?

Sammy Sheep: You're not so baaaaaad!

What did the French chef give his girlfriend on Valentine's day?

A hug and a quiche.

Why did the two bananas fall in love?

They found each other a-peel-ing!

What did the pen say to the paper?

"I dot my i's on you!"

How do loved-up hens dance?

Chick to chick!

Why does Cupid have wings?

Because "love is in the air!"

What did the rectangle write in the triangle's Valentine?

"I think you're acute!"

Why didn't the skeleton go to the Valentine Ball?

He had nobody to go with!

How much does a slobbery dog love its owner?

Drooly, madly, deeply!

How do rabbits travel on honeymoon?

On American Harelines!

What did the label say to the Champagne bottle?

"I'm stuck on you!"

Why did the couple eat fruit salad on their honeymoon?

Because they loved each other berry much.

What did the snake write in his Valentine's card?

"Love and hisses!"

How did the gorilla know about her secret admirer?

She heard it through the ape vine!

What did the worm say to its new sweetheart?

Where in earth have you been all my life?

What kind of food is best on a date?

A hearty meal!

What happened when the boxers went on a date?

It was glove at first sight!

Did you hear about the deer's relative that ran off to get married?

Antelope!

What did the sailor say to his girlfriend?

"I'm feeling quite row-mantic!"

How did the witch doctor ask the girl on a date?

"Voodoo like to go out with me?"

How did the two fortune tellers meet?

At the crystal ball!

Did you hear about the lonely zombie?

He really wanted a ghoul-friend!

Knock, knock!
Who's there?
Jimmy.
Jimmy who?
Jimmy a hug!

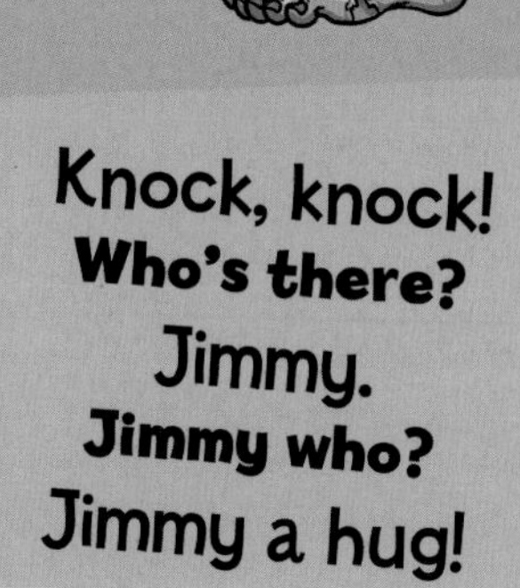

Why are tulips the best flowers to give a girl?

Because tulips are for kissing!

Why didn't the bear want to dance at the Valentine ball?

Because it had two left feet!

Where do burgers go for a Valentine's Day dance?

To the meatball!

What did the electrician say to his sweetheart?

"I love you a watt!"

Why aren't bananas ever lonely?

Because they hang out in bunches!

What did the lightbulb say to the switch?

"You light up my life!"

Why did the bats get married?

Because they were heels over heads in love!

What did the cheerleader shout to the baseball player?

"Hey, glover boy!"

What sound do porcupines make when they kiss?

Ouch!

Why did the tortoises get married?

Because they were turtle-y in love!

How did the skeleton know he had found true love?

He felt it in his bones!

What did the patient say to the fracture nurse?

"I've got a crutch on you!"

Why did the calendar feel popular?

It had plenty of dates!

Where did the cows go on their first date?

To the mooseum!

What flowers did the frog give to his girlfriend?

Croak-uses!

Knock, knock!
Who's there?
Abby.
Abby who?
Abby Valentine's Day!

What did the needle say to the button?

"I love you sew much!"

Do you love me more than you love ice cream?

I'll tell you in a minute – this cone is melting!

Where do vampires go on honeymoon?

Veinice!

Knock, knock!
Who's there?
Olive.
Olive who?
Olive you a lot!

What did the almond say to the pistachio?

"You're nut so bad you know!"

Did you hear about the cherubs that got married?

They lived harpily ever after!

How does a lemon ask for a hug?

"Give me a squeeze!"

Why did the woman marry the fisherman?

She fell for him hook, line, and sinker!

What did Frankenstein's monster write in his card?

"Be my Valenstein!"

Why did the couple honeymoon in the Arctic?

To have a really cool time!

What did one squirrel say to its sweetheart?

"I'm nuts about you!"

Knock, knock!
Who's there?
Luke.
Luke who?
Luke how many Valentines I got!

Did you hear about the loved-up bees?

They were on their honeymoon!

Who is Mom Corn's Valentine?

Pop Corn... of course!

Why did the surgeon fall in love with the generous girl?

He knew her heart was in the right place!

What does an interior decorator want on Valentine's Day?

Rugs and kisses!

What did the ghost say to his girlfriend?

"You're boo-tiful!"

What kind of flowers are no good for Valentine's Day?

Cauliflowers!

This edition created in 2016 by Arcturus Publishing Limited
26/27 Bickels Yard, 151–153 Bermondsey Street, London SE1 3HA

ISBN 978-1-78428-588-3

10 9 8 7 6 5 4 3 2 1 15 16 17 18 19

Printed in China

First Scholastic edition, Sep 2016

Supplier 29, Date 0916, Print Run 5765
CH005517US
Author: Lisa Regan
Editor: Joe Harris
Designer: Trudi Webb

Picture Credits:
All illustrations courtesy of Shutterstock